PURPOSED TO DOMINATE

DARLENE BELL

DARLENE BELL
PURPOSED TO DOMINATE
"Discover your Territory, Build your Capacity, &
Multiply your GOD-GIVEN Assignment!"

This book is published by **Darlene Bell Ministries**.

For speaking engagements, ministry inquiries, or additional resources, please contact:

Darlene Bell Ministries

First Edition

Printed in the United States of America

Dedication This book is dedicated to God, the Author of purpose and the Giver of dominion. Thank You, Lord, for trusting me with vision, assignment, and the responsibility to steward what You have placed within me. To every reader who holds this book may you discover the strength within you to walk boldly in your God-given territory, build with wisdom, and produce fruit that remains. And to those who have supported, prayed, and believed in the calling on my life, thank you for being part of the journey. My Mother, The Late Annie Gail. I would also like to dedicate this book to My daughter Jayla White Davis she has been my motivation throughout this whole process.

To my mother, whose strength was the wind beneath my wings.

You lived with a determination that never bent, a resilience that taught me how to rise, and a faith that showed me how to stand firm. Your life was my first lesson in courage, perseverance, and purpose. I am who I am because you refused to let life break you.

And to my daughter, Jayla

the continuation of that legacy.

Your light, your fire, and your quiet strength remind me that what my mother poured into me now flows into you. You inspire me to keep becoming, keep growing, and keep walking boldly in the calling God placed on my life.

Darlene Bell Ministries Mission

Darlene Bell Ministries exists to inspire, equip, and empower individuals to discover their purpose, strengthen their faith, and walk boldly in their God-given assignment.

Through teaching, mentorship, and spiritual development, this ministry seeks to help people grow in wisdom, discipline, leadership, and spiritual maturity so they can influence their families, communities, and spheres of responsibility with integrity and excellence.

Our mission is to help believers align their lives with God's Word, develop strong character, and build lives that produce lasting fruit and generational impact.

About the Author

Darlene Bell is a leader, author, and visionary committed to helping others discover their purpose and walk confidently in their God-given assignment.

Through Darlene Bell Ministries, she teaches principles of faith, leadership, personal development, and spiritual growth that empower individuals to live with clarity, discipline, and dominion.

Her passion is to see people break cycles of limitation, strengthen their capacity, and build lives that produce lasting fruit and generational impact.

Darlene believes that when individuals align their hearts with God's purpose and steward their gifts faithfully, they can influence their families, communities, and industries in powerful ways.

Her message centers on faith, responsibility, and the call to walk boldly in the territory God has assigned.

Through her writing and ministry, Darlene continues to encourage others to grow, build, and multiply what God has placed within them.

Foreword

It is both an honor and a blessing to introduce this book written by someone I deeply admire my mother.

Growing up, I had the privilege of witnessing her faith, strength, and perseverance up close. Life has not always been easy for her, but through every challenge, every obstacle, and every season, I watched her stand firm in her belief that God always has the final say. She has never been someone who simply talks about faith she lives it.

This book, *Purposed to Dominate*, is more than words on pages. It is the story of a woman who has walked through trials, learned the power of prayer, and discovered that God never intended for His people to live defeated lives. Instead, we are called to rise, to walk in purpose, and to operate in the authority God has given us.

What makes this message so powerful is that it comes from a real place. My mother has prayed through hard seasons, trusted God when things didn't make sense and learned how to stand in faith when circumstances tried to say otherwise. Her story is a reminder that no matter where you come from or what you have faced, God has a plan for your life.

In this book, you will not only read her testimony, but you will also learn practical ways to strengthen your prayer life, trust God more deeply, and walk boldly in the purpose He has placed inside of you.

My prayer is that as you read these pages, you will be encouraged, strengthened, and reminded that you were never created to live beneath what God has called you to. You were created with purpose, and through Christ, you are empowered to dominate every obstacle that stands in your way.

I am incredibly proud of the woman she is, the faith she carries, and the lives that will be impacted by this message.

May this book bless you, strengthen your faith, and remind you of the power that comes from trusting God completely.

Jayla White Davis

Author's Note

This book was written from a place of revelation, prayer, and personal growth.

Throughout my journey, I began to understand that God did not call His people simply to exist, but to walk in dominion with responsibility, wisdom, and faith.

Dominion is not about control or status. It is about stewardship governing what God has entrusted to us with discipline, integrity, and obedience.

My prayer is that as you read these pages, you will begin to see your life differently. That your thinking will expand, your capacity will grow, and your faith will deepen.

You were created with purpose.
You were designed to bear fruit.
And in your God-assigned territory, you are called to establish, build, and multiply.

May this book encourage you to align your heart with God's plan and walk confidently in the assignment He has placed upon your life.

— **Darlene Bell**

Introduction

There comes a moment in every person's life when they realize they were created for more.

More purpose.
More responsibility.
More impact.

For many people, life becomes a cycle of survival working, striving, and hoping things will change. Deep inside, there is often a quiet knowing that God placed something greater within them.

This book was born out of that realization.

God never intended for His people to live beneath their calling. From the very beginning, in Genesis, He declared that humanity would be fruitful, multiply, and have dominion.

Dominion was not meant to be about control or power. It was meant to be about stewardship governing what God places in your hands with wisdom, discipline, and faith.

Throughout this book, you will discover that dominion begins internally before it is seen externally. Your thinking must be renewed. Your heart must be aligned. Your capacity must be strengthened. Your preparation must match your faith.

Only then can territory expand.

You will learn how to sharpen your thinking, govern your atmosphere, and develop the discipline necessary to carry the responsibility of influence.

This journey is not just about personal success. It is about building something that produces fruit, multiplies, and leaves a lasting impact.

My prayer is that as you read these pages, you begin to see yourself differently.

You are not here by accident.

You are not without purpose.

You are not limited to what you have experienced so far.

You were designed to bear fruit, build with wisdom, and walk confidently in the territory God has assigned to you.

And when purpose meets preparation, dominion becomes possible

How to Use This Book

This book is not meant to be read quickly and set aside.

It is meant to be reflected on, prayed through, and applied.

Take time to meditate on the scriptures in each chapter. Allow the principles to challenge and strengthen your thinking.

When you reach the prayer and declaration sections, speak them aloud. Confession strengthens belief, and belief shapes action.

You may also choose to revisit certain chapters during seasons of growth, transition, or decision-making.

My prayer is that this book becomes more than information it becomes a guide that helps you walk confidently in the territory God has assigned to your life.

Chapter 1
A Different Beginning

From the very start, my life felt like it veered off the path most children traveled. I was the fourth of five siblings, nestled in the middle of chaos and love. At nine, my world shifted. My mother announced she was pregnant again, and not long after, I was sent to live with my grandmother.

It wasn't just a visit; it became my new life. At ten years old, I was no longer just a child I became a caretaker. My grandmother needed help with my bedridden grandfather, and I was the one chosen to provide it. The decision wasn't mine to make. I felt alone, abandoned by the parents I had always trusted to shelter me. The secrecy made it harder. My mother insisted that I not tell anyone where I lived, as if my presence in my grandmother's home was something to be ashamed of.

Each day, my mother would drop me off at her house, and I would stay until bedtime when she returned.

The isolation stung, but the teasing hurt even more. My older sister, twenty-one and still living at home, took every opportunity to remind me of my place. Her words and actions cut deeper than I could admit at the time, leaving me to wonder why I was the one sent away while she stayed.

Nights were the hardest. When I was ten, living with my grandmother and helping care for my bedridden grandfather, the weight of loneliness would settle on me like a heavy blanket. There were nights when I would cry myself to sleep, overwhelmed by the feeling of being forgotten by my parents and the struggles of a childhood that didn't feel like a childhood at all. I longed for comfort, for something to hold on to anything to remind me that I wasn't truly alone.

One day, my mother handed me a small Bible she had purchased from the dollar store. It wasn't an extravagant gesture, but it became my lifeline. Each night, I would open its pages, even though the words often seemed foreign to me, their meanings hidden behind layers of complexity that my young mind couldn't yet grasp. Still, there was something about holding that Bible, reading its verses, and feeling the weight of its message. It spoke to a part of me I didn't fully understand at the time—a part that knew there was something greater, something that called me to more.

Though I couldn't have explained it in words, I felt different, as though I wasn't meant to be confined by the circumstances of my present. That little dollar-store Bible planted a seed of hope in my heart. It whispered to me in its own way: You are called for something more. As the years passed, the feeling that I was different called to something more never faded. Yet, I faced barriers that seemed determined to hold me back. In school, I struggled with comprehension and focus. My teacher saw my difficulties but didn't seem to care enough to help me overcome them. Instead, I felt ignored, neglected not only by my family but now by the very people who were supposed to guide me.

I was misunderstood. To some, I was just another child who couldn't keep up. They told me college wasn't an option for me, that I should focus on learning a trade. Their words stung, but somewhere deep inside, I knew they were wrong. My mother believed in me, and though her resources were limited, she found a way to invest in my future. She paid for tutoring when I was in the fifth grade, and I stayed in the program all the way until eighth grade.

The hours spent with a tutor were my turning point. Slowly, I began to see improvement. With time, my grades climbed, and my confidence began to grow. High school brought new challenges, but by then, I had learned to push myself harder than I ever thought possible. I refused to be limited by the expectations others had placed on me. I was determined to reach further than anyone thought I could.

Determined to Rise

Graduating high school had been a triumph in itself, but I knew I wanted more. College seemed like the next step, a chance to break free from the limitations I'd faced. But once again, reality struck. My father refused to pay for my education, citing his income as the reason I couldn't qualify for federal funding. He made it clear that he wouldn't cover the costs himself. It felt like another door closing, another dream slipping out of reach.

Determined not to let this setback define my future, I took a job at the hospital and began paying for school on my own. I pursued nursing but struggled to pass the nursing test, a failure that stung deeply. Instead of giving up, I turned to a trade, still believing there was more within me. Over time, I found my way back to school and became an OB-GYN tech. It wasn't the destination I'd imagined, but it brought me closer to where I wanted to be. I worked my way into a better position at the hospital, constantly striving, always reaching for more.

But life has a way of testing us when we least expect it. At 24, I found out I was pregnant. A year later, I gave birth to my daughter a beautiful baby girl who became my everything. Her father enlisted in the military to help provide for her, but when he returned, life took him down a darker path. He got involved in trouble and eventually ended up in prison, leaving me to raise our daughter as a single parent.

It was a new kind of challenge, but the fire within me never dimmed. I was her mother, her provider, her protector, and her guide. No matter how hard life became, I knew I had to keep pushing forward for her and for myself.

Life shifted once again when I began working at a new hospital. It was there that I encountered a group of younger women who introduced me to Jesus. At first, I brushed off their words. Faith wasn't something I was ready to embrace I had been through so much that loneliness and struggle felt like constants in my life. Raising my daughter as a single mother while her father served time in prison weighed heavily on me.

But as time went on, their words started to resonate. I found myself drawn to the promise of comfort and peace they spoke about. It wasn't a sudden transformation it was slow, like the steady breaking of dawn. The loneliness I had carried for years began to dissipate as I sought solace in faith. Through prayer and reflection, I found Jesus in my life and became a new creature in Christ. His presence filled the emptiness I had carried and brought a light into the darkest corners of my soul.

Supporting my daughter's father while he was in prison for twenty years was not easy, but I did so with strength and love. My faith became my anchor during that time, keeping me steady even when circumstances felt overwhelming. At work, the friendships I formed with those women became a lifeline, bringing me into a community of support and compassion. Filled with the Holy Spirit, I began to thrive in ways I hadn't thought possible. Each day brought me closer to a version of myself I could finally recognize—whole, empowered, and deeply rooted in God's love. Holding On to Faith

Week after week, I visited him in prison, taking our daughter along with me. I carried hope in my heart—hope that the love of Jesus could transform his life. Each visit became a part of our journey, a way to show him the light I had found and to encourage him to embrace it. When he was finally released after twenty long years, our daughter was 21 and living her own life for Jesus. I believed in new beginnings and wanted desperately for our family to work.

But life doesn't always follow the path we envision. The weight of betrayal shattered my dream of reconciliation, and we broke up. The pain was devastating, a crushing blow to my spirit. As if the heartache weren't enough, I also lost the home I had worked so hard to purchase. For a week, my daughter and I were homeless, left to navigate a world that suddenly felt harsh and unforgiving.

Despite everything, I clung tightly to my faith. I kept telling myself telling both of us that God had more for us. Even in the depths of brokenness, I held on to the belief that this wasn't the end of our story. The challenges tested me in ways I had never imagined, but they also strengthened my resolve. With my daughter by my side, we chose to keep the faith, knowing that brighter days lay ahead.

A Reset

Finding a place to rent marked the beginning of a new chapter in my life a chance to rebuild my heart and mend the brokenness I had carried for so long. It wasn't easy, but every step felt like a piece of healing. Then, the devastating pandemic of 2020 arrived, and the world shifted in ways no one could have anticipated. At the time, I was working as a social service director in a nursing home, a position that brought mounting pressure and challenges as the virus spread fear and uncertainty through every corner of life.

Even as the weight of this job pressed down on me, I felt a stirring deep within, reminding me that I was called for more. Since 2015, I had been working on a case management business an idea that had been sitting on the shelf of my life, waiting for the right moment. That moment came in the form of an inspired word from God. I felt His guidance to leave my job, give two weeks' notice, and finally pursue the business I had dreamed of for so long. It was a leap of faith, one that carried both hope and fear.

September brought the start of this new journey, but life didn't suddenly become easy. The challenges remained, and the uncertainty of the pandemic added to my worries. Yet, before the pandemic, an evangelist visited my church and shared a prophecy with me. He told me that the Lord said I would no longer have a broken heart, and he made it clear this message came from God. That day marked a turning point. I became stronger and stronger, holding on to the promise of healing and restoration.

While the pandemic brought fear, it also brought trust a reliance on God to carry me through this reset in my life. Every day was a reminder that faith could outshine even the darkest of times.

Chapter 2
Subdue The Market

Subduing the Market

The next word the Holy Spirit revealed to me was subdue. At first, I meditated on its meaning, wondering how it applied to my journey. Then, it became clear: God was calling me to control the market; to walk in authority and confidently take ownership of the space He had entrusted to me.

To subdue wasn't about overpowering, it was about mastering. I needed to learn everything I could about my field, my business, and the market I was entering. This wasn't a passive calling; it was an active one. It required me to step boldly into the opportunities God had placed before me, to claim them as my own, and to set a standard for excellence that others could follow.

God began to show me that subduing the market wasn't just about success; it was about stewardship. By taking control and thriving, I could create opportunities for others, bless those around me, and honor the gifts God had placed within me. It was a call to dominate in faith, wisdom, and skill—not for personal glory, but for the glory of God and the betterment of His Kingdom.

This word ignited a fire in me to not only pursue my dreams but to pursue them with purpose and authority. It was a reminder that I wasn't just called to be part of the market. I was called to subdue it and make an impact that would ripple far beyond my own reach. The Power of the Tongue

As my journey continued, I discovered the incredible power of the tongue. The Bible says in Proverbs 18:21, "Death and life are in the power of the tongue." Those words took root in my heart and became a guiding principle in how I spoke about my business and my future. I realized that the words I chose could either build up or tear down. They could bring life to my dreams or speak death over them.

I began to direct my tongue with intention, choosing to believe for more and to declare positivity over my business. No longer would I allow doubt or negativity to creep into my speech. Instead, I proclaimed growth, success, and abundance over my work. With each declaration, I felt a shift not just in my mindset, but in the results I saw.

My business began to grow, reflecting the life-giving words I had spoken over it. I learned that controlling my tongue wasn't just about discipline; it was about aligning my words with God's promises. Speaking positively became an act of faith, a way of partnering with God to bring His will into reality.

This chapter in my journey wasn't just about business it was a lesson in the power of faith-filled speech and the fruits it can yield.

When God Began to Rebuild Me

Finding a place to live after losing everything felt like stepping onto shaky ground. I was grateful, but I was also exhausted. I had been fighting for so long that survival had become my normal. But God was about to show me that survival was not my destiny, transformation was.

In that small home, God began to peel back layers I didn't even know were there. He exposed wounds I had learned to function with. He revealed fears I had disguised as strength. He showed me the places where I had settled for less because I didn't believe I deserved more.

It wasn't always comfortable, but it was necessary.

I cried. I prayed. I surrendered. I healed.

Piece by piece, God rebuilt me not into who I used to be, but into who I was always meant to be.

The Awakening of Purpose

As I healed, something awakened inside me a fire, a vision, a sense of calling that had been buried under years of struggle. I realized that everything I had survived wasn't random. It was training. Preparation. Refining.

I began to feel a pull toward helping others.

A desire to speak life into women who felt unseen.

A passion to guide people through the same storms I had weathered.

A hunger to build something that would outlive my pain.

I didn't know the full picture yet, but I knew God was calling me higher.

I started dreaming again.

I started planning again.

I started believing again.

And for the first time in a long time, I felt alive.

Stepping Into Leadership

At work, people began to notice the change in me. I wasn't just showing up I was shining. I was encouraging others, uplifting them, praying for them, and speaking life into their situations. Women who were struggling came to me for guidance. Younger staff looked to me for direction. Even supervisors trusted me with more responsibility.

I didn't ask for leadership it found me.

God was showing me that influence isn't about titles. It's about impact. It's about presence. It's about the oil you carry.

And the oil on my life was beginning to flow.

The Birth of a Vision

As I continued to grow spiritually, God began to reveal the blueprint of my future. I saw glimpses of:

- a nonprofit that would empower women
- a business that would serve families with compassion
- a ministry that would heal hearts
- a book that would speak truth and transformation

I didn't know how it would all come together, but I knew it would. God had taken me from brokenness to boldness, from homelessness to hope, from pain to purpose.

A New Strength Rising

The more I leaned into God, the more confident I became. Not in myself — but in Him. I realized that every setback had strengthened me. Every heartbreak had humbled me. Every loss had taught me. Every tear had watered the seeds of my destiny.

I was no longer the woman who struggled to find her place.

I was no longer the woman who settled for survival.

I was no longer the woman who questioned her worth.

I was becoming a woman of vision.

A woman of faith.

A woman of purpose.

A woman of power.

And I knew deep in my spirit — that the next chapter of my life would not be defined by what I had lost, but by what God was about to build through me.

When Purpose Found Me

As life slowly stabilized, I began to notice something shifting inside me. It wasn't loud or dramatic — it was subtle, steady, and unmistakable. It felt like God was stirring the waters of my spirit, awakening something that had been dormant for years.

For the first time, I wasn't just surviving.

I was listening.

I was watching.

I was becoming.

Every hardship I had endured — the rejection, the single motherhood, the heartbreak, the homelessness, the long years of visiting the prison — began to feel like pieces of a larger puzzle. I realized that God had been shaping me through every season, preparing me for something far greater than I could see.

Purpose wasn't something I chased purpose was something that found me and I'm glad about it.

Chapter 3
Called to Dominate

Starting my business felt like a leap of faith, but it was a journey I knew I had to take. At home, I poured my energy into turning my dream into a reality. However, reality hit hard when I quickly ran out of funds. The initial denial of my business application stung, but giving up wasn't an option. I was determined that this dream had to work. I went back to the drawing board, completing each step with renewed purpose, and eventually, my persistence paid off I was approved, and my business was finally set up.

But now came the real challenge: finding clients. The road ahead seemed daunting, but I wasn't alone. My daughter became my greatest motivator, cheering me on and reminding me to keep going. Her encouragement, paired with my unshakable faith, propelled me forward. I turned to the Word of God for guidance, finding a sturdy foundation in His promises.

This book was born from that journey. God began to speak to me through scripture, revealing truths that would shape not only my business but my entire outlook on life. The words of Genesis 1:26-28 resonated deeply "Be fruitful, multiply, replenish, subdue it, and dominate." These verses became more than just words they became my calling.

Through prayer and study, I realized I was created not to merely survive, but to thrive and dominate in every area of my life. The struggles, the setbacks, and even the moments of doubt were all part of the process. God was showing me how to step into the fullness of who He had called me to be.

The Call to Be Fruitful

The first command God gave to man was clear: "Be fruitful." Those words carried profound meaning an instruction to be productive, to create, and to bring forth something meaningful. For me, this wasn't just a spiritual mandate; it became a guiding principle for my life and my business.

As I studied God's word, I began to see this command in a new light. Being fruitful meant producing something that had value, something that could make an impact. With this truth in my heart, I revisited my business plan with renewed purpose. I wasn't just creating a business I was stepping into alignment with what God had called me to do. This wasn't about simply earning a living; it was about fulfilling a divine directive.

I poured my faith into every step, believing that God would bless my efforts and make my business productive. It wasn't always easy, but the belief that I was walking in obedience to His word gave me strength and determination. Each day, I held on to the promise that as I worked and trusted in Him, my business would bear fruit not just for my family, but for His glory.

The first command God gave to man was clear: "Be fruitful." Those words carried profound meaning an instruction to be productive, to create, and to bring forth something meaningful. For me, this wasn't just a spiritual mandate; it became a guiding principle for my life and my business.

As I studied God’s word, I began to see this command in a new light. Being fruitful meant producing something that had value, something that could make an impact. With this truth in my heart, I revisited my business plan with renewed purpose. I wasn’t just creating a business I was stepping into alignment with what God had called me to do. This wasn’t about simply earning a living; it was about fulfilling a divine directive.

I poured my faith into every step, believing that God would bless my efforts and make my business productive. It wasn’t always easy, but the belief that I was walking in obedience to His word gave me strength and determination. Each day, I held on to the promise that as I worked and trusted in Him, my business would bear fruit not just for my family, but for His glory.

Genesis 1:26 is a pivotal verse in the Bible that reveals God's purpose for humanity. It states:

"And God said, let us make man in our image, after our likeness: and let them have dominion over the fish of the sea, and over the fowl of the air, and over the cattle, and over all the earth, and over every creeping thing that creped upon the earth."

This verse emphasizes that humans are uniquely created in the image and likeness of God, which reflects qualities like creativity, reason, and spiritual connection. It also highlights humanity's role in exercising dominion and stewardship over the earth and all living things.

As I continued to walk in faith and align myself with God's Word, the next divine directive was given to me: Multiply. This was more than just a command; it was a promise and a prophecy. The word "reproduce" resonated deeply, and I knew in my heart that God was revealing something profound about my purpose. I was called not just to produce but to reproduce to take what He had planted within me and expand it, making an impact that would stretch beyond myself.

This wasn't limited to the physical sense of reproduction; it extended into every area of life. God was calling me to multiply my influence, my legacy, and the fruits of the talents and gifts He had blessed me with. I began to see my business, my relationships, and even my faith as opportunities to multiply, to reproduce goodness, growth, and prosperity. The vision was clear: this was a season of expansion, and God had equipped me to step into it with boldness.

As I meditated on this calling, I felt a renewed sense of purpose. My work, my family, and my walk with Christ were all interconnected, forming a tapestry of multiplication. I trusted God's promise and began to move forward, believing that He was guiding me to reproduce His love and blessings in the world around me.

Called to Replenish

The next word the Holy Spirit gave me was replenishing. It wasn't just a word it was an assignment. As I meditated on its meaning, God began to reveal to me that replenishing wasn't solely about restoring; it was about becoming a distribution center, a conduit through which His blessings could flow to others. This revelation deeply resonated with me. I realized I wasn't just meant to receive abundance I was called to share it, to pour into others, and to ensure that resources, love, and hope were continually distributed.

God's plans for me began to unfold in ways I hadn't imagined. I could see how the business He had placed on my heart was meant to be a tool for replenishing, not only in financial terms but in providing opportunities, support, and inspiration to others. This was bigger than just me this was a divine calling to ensure that His blessings didn't stop with me but flowed through me to uplift those around me.

Through prayer and study, I began to understand that true fulfillment came not from holding onto what I had but from releasing it, from trusting God to continually replenish me so that I could replenish others. This new perspective filled me with purpose and determination, igniting a fire in me to walk boldly in this calling.

The Power of Reproduction

As I continued to seek God's guidance in my life and my work, I received another word from the Holy Spirit: "What you can't reproduce, dies." These words pierced my heart with their truth. I realized that reproduction wasn't just about multiplying for my own benefit—it was about ensuring that the blessings and purpose God had placed in me didn't stop with me. If I couldn't reproduce what God had given me, its impact would end when I did. But if I reproduced, it would live on, expanding and thriving far beyond my lifetime.

This revelation set my heart ablaze with a renewed sense of urgency. My dreams, my business, my faith everything God had planted within me was meant to be reproduced, to impact others and continue the cycle of abundance and purpose. It wasn't just about building something for myself; it was about creating something that could inspire, equip, and bless others for generations to come. I began to think differently, approaching my work and my life with the mindset of reproduction and legacy.

I trusted God to guide me, knowing that He had called me not only to be fruitful and multiply but also to ensure that the seeds I planted would continue to grow, thrive, and bless others. This truth became a cornerstone of my journey, driving me to live with purpose and to honor the gifts God had placed within me.

How Words Shape Identity, Atmosphere, and Spiritual Alignment

Identity: Words Become Mirrors

Words don't just describe us they form us.

Every declaration becomes a brushstroke on the canvas of who we believe we are. When someone repeatedly hears "you're strong," "you're capable," or "you're chosen," those words begin to settle into the bones. They shape self-perception, confidence, and the internal narrative that guides decisions.

But the opposite is also true.

Negative words can distort identity, shrink potential, and create internal ceilings. Many people are not fighting demons they're fighting definitions spoken over them.

Identity is built from:

- The words we speak to ourselves
- The words spoken over us
- The words we choose to accept or reject

When we speak life, we reinforce truth. When we speak death, we reinforce limitation. Identity is always under construction, and words are the builders.

The Birth of Daughter of Grace

It started as a whisper a desire to help women who felt broken, overlooked, or forgotten. Women who carried silent battles. Women who needed someone to speak life into them. Women who needed what I had needed for so long: hope, guidance, and a safe place to heal.

I didn't have a blueprint.

I didn't have funding.

I didn't have connections.

But I had a testimony.

I had compassion.

I had a calling.

And God took those three things and breathed vision into them.

Daughter of Grace was born out of my own ashes a ministry for women who needed to know that God could still use them, still love them, still restore them, still raise them up. It became a place where brokenness met purpose, where pain met healing, where women discovered their identity in Christ.

I didn't know it then, but this was the beginning of my life's work.

Heaven Sent Case Management: Purpose in the Marketplace

As I continued to grow spiritually, God began to show me that ministry wasn't limited to the church. It could live in the workplace. It could live in service. It could live in compassion.

I had always been drawn to helping people advocating for them, supporting them, guiding them through difficult systems. My own experiences with struggle made me sensitive to the needs of others. I understood what it felt like to be overlooked, unheard, or unsupported.

That's when the idea for Heaven Sent Case Management began to form.

It wasn't just a business it was a calling. A way to serve families with dignity. A way to bring compassion into healthcare. A way to create jobs and opportunities for others. A way to build something that reflected God's heart.

I didn't realize it at the time, but God was positioning me to become a leader, an entrepreneur, and a vessel of healing in the community.

The Woman I Was Becoming

As these visions unfolded, I began to see myself differently. I wasn't the girl who struggled to pass nursing exams anymore. I wasn't the young mother fighting to survive. I wasn't the woman who lost her home. I wasn't the woman who cried in silence.

I was becoming a woman of influence.

A woman of purpose.

A woman of faith.

A woman of resilience.

A woman who could turn pain into power.

Everything I had gone through had prepared me for this moment. The storms didn't break me they built me. The losses didn't destroy me they refined me. The heartbreak didn't end me it awakened me.

I was stepping into a version of myself I had never met before, but one God had always known.

With my daughter grown and thriving in her own walk with Jesus, I felt a freedom I had never experienced. I knew deep in my spirit that God was not finished with me. He was just getting started.

This was the beginning of the woman who would one day:

- lead teams
- build businesses
- mentor women
- write books
- speak life
- create change
- walk boldly in her calling

Chapter 4
The Power of the Tongue

As I stepped into this new season of purpose, I began to realize something profound: everything I had survived, everything I had built, and everything God was calling me to do had one common thread my words.

Looking back, I could see how the things I spoke in my darkest moments shaped the path before me. When I said, “I will make it,” I did. When I declared, “My daughter will rise,” she did. When I whispered, “God has more for us,” He revealed it. Even when I was broken, even when I was homeless, even when I was heartbroken, my mouth refused to agree with defeat.

I didn’t understand it then, but I was practicing a spiritual law without knowing its name.

My tongue was building the life I was walking into.

Every declaration became a stepping stone.

Every prayer became a lifeline.

Every word of faith became a seed.

Every refusal to speak negativity became a shield.

And as God elevated me as a mother, a woman, a leader, and a builder. He began to show me the truth I had lived without realizing:

Your life will always move in the direction of your words.

The same mouth that cried in pain also prophesied my future.

The same voice that trembled in fear also spoke victory.

The same woman who once felt powerless discovered that her greatest power had been with her all along.

It wasn't money that carried me. It wasn't connections. It wasn't luck. It was the power of the tongue the ability to speak life when everything around me looked like death.

This revelation changed everything.

It changed how I spoke to myself. It changed how I spoke to my daughter. It changed how I spoke about my future. It changed how I prayed, how I believed, and how I built. I realized that God had not only rescued me God had trained me.

He had taught me how to use my voice as a weapon, a tool, and a compass, and as I stepped into the fullness of my calling, I knew it was time to share this truth with others. Not as a theory. Not as a cliché. But as a woman who lived it, survived it, and rose because of it.

This is where the next chapter begins. This is where I teach you what life taught me. This is where I show you how your words shape your world. This is where you discover the spiritual law that changed my life forever.

Words Shape Identity and identity is not formed in silence. It is shaped by language spoken, heard, repeated, and believed.

Long before you ever make a decision, your words have already built the framework you will live inside. What you say about yourself becomes the blueprint your life follows. I didn't understand this when I was younger. I thought identity came from what people did to me, what I survived, or what I lacked. God showed me something deeper:

Identity is built by agreement. And agreement is expressed through words.

When I spoke defeat, I lived defeated.

When I spoke fear, I lived fearful.

When I spoke strength, I lived strengthened.

When I spoke faith, I lived forward.

Your tongue is the architect of your identity.

Every sentence is a brick. Every declaration is a beam. Every confession is a foundation. If you want to change your life, you must first change your language.

Words Create Atmosphere

Words don't just shape who you are they shape the world around you.

Every room carries a climate.

Every home carries a tone.

Every relationship carries a sound.

And the tongue is the thermostat.

I learned this the hard way. There were seasons when my home felt heavy, not because of what was happening, but because of what was being spoken. Stress has a sound. Fear has a sound. Worry has a sound. But so does peace. So does gratitude. So does faith.

When I began speaking differently, my atmosphere shifted.

My home felt lighter.

My mind felt clearer.

My spirit felt steadier.

I realized that I didn't have to accept the atmosphere I could create it.

Your words can calm storms or start them. They can build bridges or burn them they can open doors or close them atmosphere is not accidental it is cultivated by the tongue words Reveal Spiritual Alignment your mouth is a spiritual compass.

It reveals what your heart has agreed with heaven or fear, faith or wounds, truth or trauma.

I used to think alignment was about behavior. But God showed me that alignment begins with language. Your words reveal what you believe, even when your mind hasn't caught up yet.

Fear speaks in one direction.

Faith speaks in another.

When I began aligning my words with God's promises instead of my pain, everything shifted. My prayers changed. My confidence changed. My decisions changed. My future changed.

Your tongue positions your spirit.

Your spirit positions your life.

This is why the enemy doesn't need to silence your feet he only needs to silence your mouth. Because if he can control your confession, he can influence your direction.

Once you learn to speak with authority, heaven backs you.

Once you learn to speak with faith, mountains move.

Once you learn to speak with truth, chains break.

This is the power of the tongue and it is the foundation of every transformation you will ever experience.

Words Create Climate

Words don't just stay inside a person they fill a room.

They shift the emotional temperature of a home, workplace, or relationship. A single sentence can calm a storm or start one. A gentle word can soften tension. A harsh word can ignite conflict.

Atmospheres respond to language:

- Encouraging words create safety
- Critical words create anxiety
- Grateful words create peace
- Complaining words create heaviness

- Visionary words create momentum

People often pray for peace while speaking chaos.

They want joy while releasing negativity.

They desire unity while sowing division with their tongue.

Atmosphere is not accidental it is cultivated, and the primary tool of cultivation is speech.

Spiritual Alignment: Words Position the Heart

Words don't just affect the natural realm they influence the spiritual one.

Speech reveals alignment whether a person is speaking from fear or faith, from wounds or wisdom, from flesh or spirit.

Words can:

- Pull a person back into alignment with purpose
- Disconnect them from distractions
- Anchor them in truth
- Invite clarity
- Strengthen discernment

When someone speaks faith-filled words, they align themselves with what God has already spoken. When they speak doubt, they align with what circumstances are trying to dictate.

Spiritual alignment is not just about belief it's about agreement.

And agreement is expressed through words.

Identity is internal atmosphere is external alignment is spiritual, but the tongue touches all three.

Your words:

- Shape who you become
- Shape the environment you live in
- Shape the direction your spirit leans toward

This is why controlling the tongue is not optional — it is foundational.

It is the difference between living by design or by default.

The Creative Power of Words Identity, Atmosphere, and Alignment

Every word we speak carries weight. It either builds or breaks, plants or uproots, aligns or disrupts. Words are not casual—they are spiritual instruments. They shape how we see ourselves, how we experience the world around us, and how closely we walk with God's intention for our lives.

Let's explores the three realms your words influence every single day:

identity, atmosphere, and spiritual alignment.

Identity: Words Become Internal Architecture

Identity is not formed in silence.

It is shaped by language—spoken, heard, repeated, and believed.

The Words We Hear Become the Words We Live

From childhood, identity is constructed through phrases:

- "You're smart."
- "You're too much."
- "You'll never change."
- "You're chosen."

Some words become chains.

Some become wings.

Many adults are still living under labels they never agreed to but never challenged. Words spoken in anger, fear, or ignorance can linger for decades if they are not uprooted.

God's Pattern: He Speaks Identity Before Assignment

Before Jeremiah was a prophet, God called him one.

Before Gideon fought, God called him "mighty man of valor."

Before Jesus performed miracles, the Father declared, "This is my beloved Son."

Identity is spoken before it is lived.

Your Tongue Is a Mirror

Every time you speak about yourself, you reinforce a version of you:

- "I'm overwhelmed"
- "I'm not good enough"
- "I always mess up"

Or…

- "I'm growing"
- "I'm equipped"
- "I'm favored"
- "I'm becoming who God designed me to be"

Your words are building the person you will meet tomorrow.

Atmosphere: Words Create Climate

Words don't just shape people they shape spaces. Every Room Has a Temperature Some homes feel peaceful. Some offices feel tense. Some relationships feel heavy. Some conversations feel like fresh air. The difference is often the language spoken within them.

Words Carry Atmosphere

- Encouragement brings safety
- Gratitude brings joy
- Gossip brings suspicion
- Complaining brings heaviness

- Vision brings momentum
- Prayer brings clarity

People pray for peace while speaking chaos. They want joy while releasing negativity. They desire unity while sowing division. Atmosphere is not accidental—it is cultivated. Your Mouth Is a Thermostat, not a Thermometer. A thermometer reports the temperature a thermostat sets it.

When you walk into a room, your words can:

- calm storms
- shift tension
- break confusion
- restore hope
- create order

You don't have to accept the atmosphere you can change it.

Spiritual alignment

Words are not just emotional they are spiritual. Your Mouth Shows What Your Heart Has Agreed with Fear has a language. Faith has a language. Wounds have a language. Wisdom has a language. When you speak, you reveal which one you're aligned with.

Heaven Responds to Agreement not because your words are magic, but because your words reveal what you're partnering with.

When you speak:

- faith, you align with God
- doubt, you align with circumstances
- bitterness, you align with wounds
- truth, you align with purpose

Alignment is not just belief it is agreement. Agreement is expressed through words. Your Words Pull You into Position Sometimes your spirit is ahead of your emotions. Sometimes your emotions are ahead of your faith. Sometimes your faith is ahead of your reality. Words bring them into alignment.

Chapter 5

My Confession Positioned Me

Scripture Foundation

Proverbs 18:21 (KJV)
"Death and life are in the power of the tongue: and they that love it shall eat the fruit thereof."

Romans 10:10 (KJV)
"For with the heart man believeth unto righteousness; and with the mouth confession is made unto salvation."

Mark 11:23 (KJV)
"For verily I say unto you, that whosoever shall say unto this mountain, be thou removed, and be thou cast into the sea; and shall not doubt in his heart, but shall believe that those things which he saith shall come to pass; he shall have whatsoever he saith."

2 Corinthians 4:13 (KJV)
"We having the same spirit of faith... we also believe, and therefore speak."

There was a season in my life when I realized that what I was saying did not match what I was praying for.

I was asking God for increase, but speaking lack.
I was believing for promotion, but confessing frustration.
I was declaring purpose, but rehearsing problems.

And then something shifted.

When I learned to confess the Word of God over my life intentionally, consistently, and specifically, I began to see tangible change take place. Not overnight — but undeniably. My atmosphere shifted. My confidence shifted. My decisions shifted. And eventually, my circumstances shifted.

That was the revelation:

My confessions were positioning me.

The Power of Spoken Alignment

The Word stopped being information and became instruction.

I realized that my mouth was not just expressing how I felt it was directing where I was going. Every confession was a seed. Every declaration was construction. Every word was building something either my limitation or my legacy.

When I began to confess:

"I am called."
"I am equipped."
"I am disciplined."
"I am a wise steward."
"I walk in favor."
"I operate in excellence."

I wasn't trying to convince God.
I was aligning myself.

Confession is not about persuading Heaven it's about positioning yourself on Earth.

Confession Creates Position

Your position in life is rarely accidental. It is often the result of repeated agreements.

For years, I unknowingly agreed with fear, doubt, and delay through my words. But when I started agreeing with God's Word instead, my position changed.

I didn't just feel more confident I became more confident. I didn't just desire leadership I stepped into leadership. I didn't just pray for expansion I prepared for expansion.

My confessions disciplined my mindset. My mindset shaped my decisions. My decisions determined my position, and that's when I understood "Your confession determines your capacity".

Specific Confessions Produce Specific Results

Vague confessions produce vague results.

It wasn't enough to say, "God bless me."
I had to say:

"Lord, make me a disciplined businesswoman."
"Give me strategy to grow."
"I attract divine partnerships."
"I manage money with wisdom."
"My business is structured and sustainable."

When I became specific with my confessions, I became specific with my actions. And clarity creates momentum.

Faith is not passive agreement it is spoken alignment followed by disciplined obedience.

From Words to Position

I stand today in positions I once only spoke about.

Not because I was the most qualified.
Not because everything was easy.
But because I refused to speak beneath my calling.

I learned:

You cannot consistently speak small and expect to live large.
You cannot confess confusion and walk in clarity.
You cannot rehearse defeat and occupy dominion.

My confessions brought me to my positions.

Speak what God said.
Agree with Heaven.
Declare before you see it.
Align before you manifest it.

Because when your mouth aligns with your assignment, your life begins to move accordingly.

Prophetic Confession Declaration

Speak This Aloud

Today, I come into agreement with the Word of God concerning my life.

I declare that death and life are in the power of my tongue, and I choose to speak life.

I will no longer speak beneath my calling.
I will no longer rehearse fear, lack, delay, or limitation.
I will no longer partner with doubt through my words.

I align my mouth with Heaven.

I declare:

I am called.
I am chosen.
I am equipped for every assignment placed on my life.
I am disciplined and consistent.
I am a wise steward over every resource entrusted to me.
I operate in excellence and integrity.
Favor surrounds me like a shield.
Doors of opportunity open before me.
Divine connections locate me.
Strategy flows to me.
Clarity governs me.
Peace anchors me.

Purposed to Dominate

I declare that my business is structured and sustainable.
My leadership is impactful and influential.
My household is blessed and ordered.
My mind is sharp.
My spirit is aligned.
My steps are ordered by the Lord.

I declare that what I speak in faith positions me in reality.

Mountains move at the sound of my obedience.
Cycles are broken by my agreement with truth.
Delay is replaced with divine timing.
Confusion is replaced with clarity.
Scarcity is replaced with abundance.

I will speak what God has said — even before I see it.

I declare that my confessions are building my future.
My words are shaping my capacity.
My mouth is positioning me for dominion.

I align before I manifest.
I govern my atmosphere.
I walk in authority.

And from this day forward,

My confession will match my calling.
My words will match my destiny.
And my position will reflect my obedience.

In Jesus' name,
Amen.

Chapter 6

Dominion Is a Responsibility

Scripture Foundation

Genesis 1:26 (KJV)
"And God said, let us make man in our image, after our likeness: and let them have dominion..."

Romans 5:17 (KJV)
"...they which receive abundance of grace and of the gift of righteousness shall reign in life by one, Jesus Christ."

Luke 12:48 (KJV)
"...For unto whomsoever much is given, of him shall be much required."

There was a time when I believed dominion meant power.

I thought it meant influence. Visibility. Elevation.
I thought it meant being recognized as a leader and occupying spaces of authority.

But as I grew in maturity spiritually and practically I began to understand something deeper:

Dominion is not a privilege to enjoy.
It is a responsibility to carry.

When God gave humanity dominion in the book of Genesis, He was not creating tyrants. He was establishing stewards. He was entrusting His creation to those who reflected His image. Dominion was never about ego or control. It was about governance, accountability, and order.

That revelation reshaped how I viewed leadership, business, ministry, and even my personal discipline.

Dominion is not about being in charge.
It is about being answerable.

Genesis tells us that we were made in His image before we were given dominion. That order is not accidental. Image precedes authority.

You cannot represent what you do not reflect. If dominion flows from image, then authority must mirror His nature, His order, His wisdom, His justice, His truth.

This means dominion is not sustained by charisma.
It is sustained by character.

If your integrity cannot support your influence, your authority will eventually expose you. God does not release dominion to inflate you. He releases it to mature you.

I once thought dominating in authority meant being strong in rooms. But I learned that true authority is first proven in private. You cannot dominate externally what you have not subdued internally.

Before you govern boardrooms, you must govern your mouth.
Before you lead teams, you must lead your habits.
Before you manage increase, you must manage yourself.

Dominion requires internal order.

It requires emotional discipline — not reacting to every offense.
It requires financial stewardship — not mishandling resources.
It requires time management — not wasting what you prayed for.
It requires obedience — not convenience.

God will not expand what you cannot sustain.

This is where many desire authority but resist responsibility. They want the territory without the systems. They want the influence without the structure. They want visibility without accountability.

But dominion demands structure.

Structure is not restriction.
Structure is protection.

It protects vision from chaos.
It protects people from instability.
It protects longevity from emotional decisions.

If God entrusts you with territory and you refuse to build systems, chaos will fill the space where leadership was supposed to stand.

Dominion is heavy because it requires consistent order.

Romans says we shall "reign in life."

Reigning is not dramatic. It is disciplined.

It means you do not allow fear to dictate your movement.
You do not allow insecurity to silence your voice.
You do not allow pressure to override principle.

Reigning is the daily decision to respond with wisdom instead of reacting with emotion.

Dominion is seen in restraint.
It is seen in consistency.
It is seen in integrity when no one is applauding.

It is easy to celebrate authority. It is harder to carry it faithfully.

Then there is the sobering truth of Luke 12:48 to whom much is given, much is required.

The greater the authority, the greater the accountability.

If God has given you vision, He requires discipline.
If He has given you influence, He requires integrity.
If He has given you increase, He requires stewardship.
If He has given you leadership, He requires maturity.

Dominion is sacred because it reflects trust from Heaven, and trust requires responsibility.

When God began speaking to me about dominating in authority, I realized He was not telling me to strive harder.

He was correcting my mindset.

He was saying:

Stop shrinking in places I assigned you.
Stop hesitating when I authorized you.
Stop minimizing what I entrusted to you.

Govern what I gave you.

Build what I showed you.

Protect what I placed in your hands.

Expand what I have authorized.

And steward it with integrity.

Dominion is not about overpowering people.
It is about answering to God for how you manage what He entrusted to you.

When you understand that, you stop chasing positions and start building capacity. You stop seeking applause and start strengthening structure. You stop asking permission for what Heaven has already approved.

Dominion is not a spotlight. It is a sacred trust. And when you carry it with responsibility, authority will not corrupt you it will establish you.

Chapter 7

Governing Your Atmosphere

Scripture Foundation

2 Corinthians 10:5 (KJV)
"Casting down imaginations, and every high thing that exalted itself against the knowledge of God, and bringing into captivity every thought to the obedience of Christ."

Proverbs 4:23 (KJV)
"Keep thy heart with all diligence; for out of it are the issues of life."

Dominion becomes visible in the way you manage your atmosphere.

Atmosphere is not just the air around you. It is the emotional, mental, spiritual, and relational climate that surrounds your life and leadership.

Your atmosphere determines your productivity.
It influences your decisions.
It shapes your reactions.
It affects your clarity.

And if left unchecked, it can sabotage your assignment.

Governing your atmosphere means you do not allow:

- Negative thoughts to remain unchecked.
- Toxic conversations to linger.
- Disorder to become normal.
- Emotional instability to dictate decisions.

Authority is not only demonstrated in how you lead others it is demonstrated in how you regulate environments.

You must take thoughts captive.

You must guard your heart diligently.

You must intentionally create spaces of order, peace, focus, and discipline, because what surrounds you eventually shapes you. If you tolerate chaos long enough, it will feel normal. If you allow negativity to dominate your conversations, it will weaken your conviction. If you refuse to confront dysfunction, it will eventually control your outcomes. Dominion requires atmosphere management. You cannot pray for clarity and entertain confusion. You cannot declare peace and feed anxiety. You cannot ask God for expansion while living in disorder.

Governing your atmosphere means:

You choose what stays.
You choose what goes.

You choose what influences you.
You choose what you tolerate.

And this is where authority becomes personal. It is easy to command rooms. It is harder to command your inner climate. But true dominion begins here.

When your thoughts are disciplined, your words become precise.
When your environment is structured, your productivity increases.
When your atmosphere is peaceful, your decisions become clearer.

You begin to carry authority without forcing it, because authority flows naturally from order. If dominion is responsibility, then governing your atmosphere is daily execution of that responsibility. You cannot control everything that happens around you. But you can control what you allow to remain. That is power not loud power but aligned power. And when your internal world is governed, your external world begins to respond.

Before God Enlarges Your Territory, He Strengthens Your Interior

Proverbs 4:23 (KJV)
"Keep thy heart with all diligence; for out of it are the issues of life."

Luke 16:10 (KJV)
"He that is faithful in that which is least is faithful also in much..."

3 John 1:2 (KJV)
"Beloved, I wish above all things that thou mayest prosper and be in health, even as thy soul prospereth."

We often pray for expansion larger platforms, greater influence, increased income, wider impact. But Heaven measures readiness differently than we does.

God looks inward before He expands outward.

Proverbs tell us that the issues of life flow from the heart. That means the condition of your interior life determines the condition of your external results. If your heart is unstable, your decisions will be unstable. If your thinking is fragmented, your outcomes will be fragmented.

So, before territory increases, interior must mature.

Luke 16:10 reveals a divine principle: faithfulness in small things qualifies you for larger things. That faithfulness is not only about tasks it is about internal consistency. Can you be disciplined when no one sees you? Can you be obedient when there is no applause? Can you govern your emotions when there is no audience?

Expansion without internal strength becomes exposure.

This is why some people receive increase and lose it. Their territory grew faster than their interior capacity. Influence amplified what was unhealed. Visibility exposed what was undisciplined.

But when God strengthens your interior first, expansion becomes sustainable.

3 John 1:2 makes it clear that prosperity is tied to soul health. "Even as thy soul prosper." Your outward prosperity is designed to mirror your inward condition.

If your soul is governed, your success can be trusted.

If your soul is disciplined, your influence can endure.

If your soul is aligned, your expansion will not corrupt you.

Strengthening your interior looks like:

• Developing emotional regulation.
• Establishing disciplined habits.

- Healing insecurities.
- Refining your thought patterns.
- Submitting your will to obedience.

It is less glamorous than territory, but it is more critical.

Territory tests what interior contains. When pressure comes, you will not rise to the level of your ambition. You will fall to the level of your preparation, and preparation happens internally.

Before David ruled publicly, he learned obedience privately. Before Joseph governed Egypt, his character was tested in isolation. Before Esther influenced a nation, her courage was formed in confinement.

God enlarges territory but He strengthens interior first.

Because expansion magnifies whatever is already within you.

If chaos is within you, expansion magnifies chaos.
If insecurity is within you, expansion magnifies insecurity.
If discipline is within you, expansion magnifies discipline.
If alignment is within you, expansion magnifies authority.

So, when God delays enlargement, it is often not denial. It is development. He is strengthening your interior so your exterior can sustain weight. He is deepening your roots so your branches can spread wide. He is building character, so your calling does not collapse under pressure. Before territory increases, identity must stabilize. Before platforms grow, discipline must deepen. Before influence expands, integrity must solidify. Because when your interior is strong, enlargement does not intimidate you. It simply reveals what was already built inside. And when God finally enlarges your territory, you will not scramble to adjust. You will stand already prepared.

Chapter 8

Capacity Determines Territory

Scripture Foundation

Isaiah 54:2 (KJV)
"Enlarge the place of thy tent, and let them stretch forth the curtains of thine habitations: spare not, lengthen thy cords, and strengthen thy stakes."

Matthew 25:21 (KJV)
"...thou hast been faithful over a few things, I will make thee ruler over many things..."

2 Kings 4:3 (KJV)
"Then he said, Go, borrow thee vessels abroad... even empty vessels; borrow not a few."

We often pray for larger territory. More influence. More income. More impact. More visibility. But Heaven responds to capacity. God does not expand territory based on desire alone. He expands territory based on preparedness.

Isaiah 54 does not begin with enlargement. It begins with preparation.

"Enlarge the place of thy tent... strengthen thy stakes." Before expansion comes reinforcement. Before increase comes infrastructure. Before territory grows, capacity must be developed.

Desire Does Not Equal Readiness

Many people want what they are not yet built to sustain. They desire the stage but neglect discipline. They desire influence but avoid accountability. They desire increase but lack structure. Capacity is the ability to carry weight without collapsing. If your capacity is small, your territory will remain limited not as punishment, but as protection. God will not release what will destroy you. He will not expand what you cannot manage. He will not multiply what you mishandle. He will not increase what you cannot steward. Capacity protects territory.

Territory Expands Where Faithfulness Is Proven

Matthew 25 reveals a kingdom pattern: Faithfulness over a few things qualifies you for many things. Notice the ruler over many things was first disciplined over few things. Few things test your consistency. Few things test your integrity. Few things test your stewardship. Anyone can manage abundance for a moment. Few can manage small beginnings with excellence. Capacity is built in the unseen. It is built when you show up without applause. It is built when you execute without recognition. It is built when you refine systems no one claps for. Small seasons are not delays. They are development zones.

God Fills What You Prepare

In 2 Kings 4, the widow's oil did not run out because of lack of supply. It stopped when there were no more vessels. Heaven did not limit the oil. Capacity did. The miracle flowed according to the size of preparation. That principle is sobering. God may be willing to pour more.

The question is do you have vessels ready?

Vessels represent:

• Systems
• Discipline
• Emotional stability
• Financial structure
• Leadership maturity

If you expand without vessels, increase will leak.

Strengthen Your Stakes

Isaiah says strengthen your stakes. Stakes anchor tents in storms. If you expand width without strengthening depth, storms will uproot you.

Strengthening your stakes looks like:

• Developing financial literacy before wealth increases.
• Establishing leadership protocols before teams expand.
• Building personal discipline before opportunities

multiply.
• Healing internally before influence grows publicly.

Depth stabilizes expansion. Your roots must grow deeper than your reach.

Capacity Is Internal Before It Is External

Territory is external. Capacity is internal. Territory can be given overnight.
Capacity is built over time, and if territory grows faster than capacity, pressure will expose weakness. Pressure does not create cracks.
It reveals them. So instead of asking, "When will my territory expand?"
Ask, "Where must my capacity grow?"

Growth in capacity requires:

Intentional learning.
Structured habits.
Spiritual maturity.
Emotional intelligence.
Strategic thinking.

Expansion is not accidental. It responds to readiness.

You are not limited by opportunity. You are limited by capacity. If you're thinking is small, your decisions will be small. If your discipline is inconsistent, your growth will be inconsistent. If your standards are low, your territory will mirror that standard. But when your capacity expands: Your thinking stretches. Your systems strengthen. Your leadership deepens. Your endurance increases, and territory has room to grow.

God is not withholding territory. He is building capacity. He is enlarging your thinking. He is refining your discipline. He is strengthening your stakes. Because when capacity is strong, territory becomes sustainable. And when territory is sustained, dominion becomes visible. Capacity determines territory. So, if you want more land build stronger stakes.

If you want more influence deepen your roots. If you want greater impact expand your interior. Because Heaven does not expand what is unstable. It multiplies what is prepared.

Prophetic Declaration

Lord, Increase My Capacity

Scripture Foundation

Isaiah 54:2 (KJV)
"Enlarge the place of thy tent... lengthen thy cords, and strengthen thy stakes."

Luke 16:10 (KJV)
"He that is faithful in that which is least is faithful also in much..."

3 John 1:2 (KJV)
"...that thou mayest prosper... even as thy soul prospereth."

2 Corinthians 9:8 (KJV)
"And God is able to make all grace abound toward you; that ye, always having all sufficiency in all things, may abound to every good work."

James 1:4 (KJV)
"But let patience have her perfect work, that ye may be perfect and entire, wanting nothing."

Purposed to Dominate

Today I come before You not just asking for territory but asking for transformation.

Lord, increase my capacity.

Before You enlarge my platform, enlarge my discipline.
Before You expand my influence, expand my integrity.
Before You multiply resources, multiply my wisdom.
Before You increase visibility, increase my maturity.

Your Word declares, "Strengthen thy stakes." So, I ask you to strengthen mine.

Strengthen my mind so I can think beyond limitation.
Strengthen my emotions so I can lead without reacting.
Strengthen my character so I can carry authority without corruption. Strengthen my habits so success does not outgrow my discipline.

Your Word says that if I am faithful in little, I will be trusted with much.

Teach me to be faithful in small assignments.
Teach me to steward what I already have.
Teach me to execute consistently when no one applauds.

If my territory has not expanded yet,
build my capacity until it must.

Your Word says You are able to make all grace abound toward me
so that I may abound in every good work.

Purposed to Dominate

Increase my ability to carry grace.
Increase my endurance in pressure.
Increase my wisdom in complexity.
Increase my discipline in obscurity.

Let patience have her perfect work in me.

Make me mature and entire lacking nothing internally
before I gain anything externally.

Prosper my soul first.

Prosper my thoughts.
Prosper my convictions.
Prosper my obedience.
Prosper my private life.

I do not want expansion that exceeds my preparation.
I do not want influence that outruns my integrity.
I do not want territory that collapses under pressure.

Refine me.

Remove insecurity.
Correct instability.
Expose immaturity.
Align what is out of order.

If I must be stretched, stretch me.
If I must be refined, refine me.
If I must be disciplined, discipline me.

But do not expand me beyond my strength.

Purposed to Dominate

Build me internally so that when increase comes, I am ready.

When territory expands, let my roots be deep.
When opportunity arrives, let my systems be strong.
When pressure rises, let my character be stable.

Lord, increase my capacity

For stewardship.
For responsibility.
For sustainability.
For dominion.

And when You enlarge my territory,
let it reflect the strength You built within me.

In Jesus' name,
Amen.

Chapter 9

Preparation Is Proof of Faith

Scripture Foundation

Hebrews 11:7 (KJV)
"By faith Noah, being warned of God of things not seen as yet, moved with fear, prepared an ark..."

James 2:17 (KJV)
"Even so faith, if it hath not works, is dead, being alone."

Proverbs 24:27 (KJV)
"Prepare thy work without, and make it fit for thyself in the field; and afterwards build thine house."

Isaiah 40:31 (KJV)
"...they that wait upon the Lord shall renew their strength..."

Faith is often celebrated for what it believes. But real faith is proven by what it prepares. We say we believe God for expansion. We declare increase. We prophesy territory. But preparation reveals whether we truly expect it.

Hebrews 11:7 says Noah prepared an ark for rain he had never seen.

There was no evidence of a flood. There were no clouds in the sky. There was only a word from God. And Noah's preparation was his proof of belief. He did not wait for water to start building. He built because he believed. Preparation is visible faith.

Faith Moves Before It Sees

Many people say they believe God for more — but they are not preparing for more. They want business growth but have no systems. They want ministry expansion but lack structure. They want financial increase but have no stewardship plan. Faith is not passive. James says faith without works is dead. That means belief without preparation is incomplete. If you believe God is going to enlarge you, your habits should reflect expectation. If you believe doors are opening, your skills should be sharpening. If you believe increase is coming, your systems should be strengthening. Preparation is your silent agreement with what God said.

Waiting Is Not Idleness

Isaiah says those who wait on the Lord shall renew their strength.

Waiting in the Kingdom is not inactivity. It is strengthening. It is sharpening. It is developing endurance. While you are waiting, you should be building. While you are praying, you should be planning. While you are believing, you should be structuring. Because when opportunity comes, it will not pause for your preparation. It will reveal it.

Prepare Before You Build

Proverbs 24:27 says, "Prepare thy work… and afterwards build thine house."

There is divine order. Preparation precedes construction. We often want to build first and organize later. But God's order is different. He strengthens interior before territory. He increases capacity before influence. He calls for preparation before manifestation. If you skip preparation, pressure will expose weakness. Preparation may feel slow, but it is strategic. It builds foundation. And foundations determine longevity.

What Preparation Looks Like

Preparation is not glamorous.

It is:

- Refining your skills.
- Organizing your systems.
- Healing your insecurities.
- Strengthening your discipline.
- Clarifying your vision.
- Studying your craft.
- Establishing structure.

It is doing today what aligns with tomorrow. Preparation is proof that you expect God to move. You don't prepare for what you doubt. You prepare for what you believe.

The Hard Truth

Some delays are not spiritual warfare. They are preparation seasons. God is not withholding territory. He is asking, "Are you ready?" Because when territory expands, responsibility multiplies. When influence grows, scrutiny increases. When revenue increases, stewardship is tested. If you are not prepared internally and structurally, expansion becomes pressure instead of blessing. Preparation converts pressure into promotion.

Noah built before rain. Joseph governed before promotion. David learned warfare before kingship. Preparation is never wasted. It strengthens capacity. It stabilizes character. It protects territory. it sustains dominion. If you truly believe God is enlarging you, prepare like it. Sharpen your mind.
Strengthen your discipline. Build your systems. Deepen your roots. Because faith that prepares will never be ashamed. Preparation is proof of faith. And when opportunity arrives, it will recognize the structure you built in secret.

Prophetic Declaration

I Prepare Because I Believe

Scripture Foundation

Hebrews 11:7 (KJV)
"By faith Noah... prepared an ark..."

James 2:17 (KJV)
"Faith, if it hath not works, is dead..."

Proverbs 24:27 (KJV)
"Prepare thy work... and afterwards build thine house."

Isaiah 40:31 (KJV)
"...they that wait upon the Lord shall renew their strength..."

Today I make a decision.

I will not only believe I will prepare.

I prepare because I believe.

Purposed to Dominate

I believe God is enlarging me,
so I strengthen my structure.

I believe doors are opening,
so I sharpen my skills.

I believe territory is expanding,
so I deepen my roots.

I believe influence is increasing,
so I refine my character.

Like Noah, I build before I see rain.

I will not wait for evidence to start preparing.
I will not wait for opportunity to become disciplined.
I will not wait for visibility to develop integrity.

Faith moves before it sees.

So, I move.

I organize what I have.
I steward what is in my hand.
I refine what has been entrusted to me.
I build systems that can sustain growth.

I reject passive faith.

I reject lazy expectation.

I reject the mindset that says, "I'll get ready when it comes."

Purposed to Dominate

I get ready now.

Your Word says that faith without works is dead.

So let my preparation be proof that I believe.

Let my discipline testify that I expect increase.

Let my consistency reveal that I trust Your promise.

While I wait, I strengthen.

While I pray, I plan.

While I believe, I build.

Renew my strength as I prepare.

Stabilize my emotions.
Sharpen my thinking.
Refine my systems.
Correct my inconsistencies.
Heal what could sabotage expansion.

If opportunity came today, let me be ready.

If increase arrived tomorrow, let me sustain it.

If responsibility multiplied, let me carry it with wisdom.

I prepare because I believe.

I prepare because I expect.

Purposed to Dominate

I prepare because I know that what You promised requires readiness.

When rain falls, I will not scramble.

When doors open, I will not panic.

When territory expands, I will not collapse.

I will stand prepared.

In Jesus' name,
Amen.

Sharpen My Thinking

When I say, "Sharpen my thinking," I am not just asking God to give me more ideas. I am asking Him to refine my mind so my life can carry what my prayers are asking for. Because territory does not just require an open door it requires a renewed mind. A dull mind reacts. A sharpened mind responds. A dull mind is emotional. A sharpened mind is intentional. A dull mind repeats cycles. A sharpened mind recognizes patterns and breaks them. This is why God often works on our thinking before He changes our surroundings. If He gives you new territory with old thinking, you will recreate old outcomes in a new place.

So when I pray "Sharpen my thinking," I'm asking for mental clarity, spiritual discernment, and strategic wisdom.

Sharpen My Thinking Means:

1) Upgrade how I perceive
Lord, let me see beyond what is obvious.
Let me discern what is happening underneath what is happening.
Let me recognize doors, distractions, and danger—before they manifest fully.

2) Refine how I decide
Help me move from impulsive choices to principled decisions.

Teach me to choose what is wise, not just what is easy.
Give me the discipline to delay gratification for destiny.

3) Remove mental clutter
Cluttered minds produce cluttered outcomes.
Sharpen my focus.
Silence unnecessary noise.
Teach me what deserves my attention and what drains my capacity.

4) Correct limiting beliefs
Some mindsets feel normal because they are familiar, not because they are true.
Expose every belief that contradicts Your Word.
Replace survival thinking with dominion thinking.
Replace scarcity thinking with stewardship thinking.

5) Develop strategic thinking
Lord, teach me to plan.
Teach me to build systems.
Teach me to anticipate.
Teach me to think long-term and lead with vision.

Because wisdom is not only spiritual — it is structured.

Scripture to Anchor It

Romans 12:2 (KJV)
"And be not conformed to this world: but be ye transformed by the renewing of your mind..."

2 Timothy 1:7 (KJV)
"For God hath not given us the spirit of fear; but of power, and of love, and of a sound mind."

James 1:5 (KJV)
"If any of you lack wisdom, let him ask of God..."

A sound mind is part of dominion. Sharpened thinking is proof of maturity. And here's the truth: when God sharpens your mind, He sharpens your life — because your life will only rise to the level of your thinking.

When your thinking is sharpened:

You stop misreading seasons.
You stop entertaining distractions.
You stop making decisions that sabotage your own prayers.
You begin moving with clarity, consistency, and courage.

So yes, Lord sharpen my thinking.

So I can recognize what You are doing.
So I can steward what You are sending.
So I can sustain what You are expanding.

Chapter 10

You Have What You Say

The Mouth Speaks From the Heart

Mark 11:23 (KJV)
"...he shall have whatsoever he saith."

Matthew 12:34 (KJV)
"...for out of the abundance of the heart the mouth speaketh."

Proverbs 18:21 (KJV)
"Death and life are in the power of the tongue..."

There is a divine connection between your heart, your mouth, and your manifestation. Jesus said, "He shall have whatsoever he saith." That statement is not poetic. It is principle. But many people quote Mark 11:23 without understanding Matthew 12:34. You will have what you say —
but you will say what fills your heart. Your mouth is not random. It reveals what is stored within you. If fear fills your heart, fear will fill your speech.
If insecurity fills your heart, insecurity will fill your speech. If faith fills your heart, faith will fill your speech. If confidence fills your heart, authority will fill

your speech. The mouth is the overflow system of the heart.

So, when Scripture says you will have what you say, it is not encouraging careless talking — it is revealing a cycle:

Heart → Mouth → Manifestation.

What lives in your heart eventually exits through your mouth. What exits your mouth eventually shapes your reality.

This is why sharpening your thinking matters. Because thoughts feed the heart. The heart fuels the mouth. The mouth frames the future. If your internal world is ungoverned, your words will betray you. You may pray for increase but constantly speak struggle. You may declare dominion but rehearse limitation. You may ask God for expansion but confess exhaustion, doubt, and defeat. And your life will respond to the loudest agreement — not the quietest prayer.

The Abundance Principle

"Out of the abundance of the heart…"

Abundance means overflow. Whatever you meditate on consistently becomes your internal abundance. If you constantly rehearse past failures, failure becomes abundant. If you constantly focus on lack, lack becomes abundant.

If you constantly meditate on God's promises, faith becomes abundant. And whatever becomes abundant will speak without effort. You do not have to force what is truly in your heart. It will surface under pressure. Pressure reveals abundance.

When stress comes, what spills out?
Faith or fear?
Vision or victimhood?
Clarity or chaos?

Your words under pressure expose your heart's condition. That is why governing your atmosphere and strengthening your interior is critical. Because if your heart is aligned, your mouth will align naturally.

You Frame What You Live In

Hebrews 11:3 says the worlds were framed by the Word of God.

Words frame worlds.

And while we do not create like God creates, we participate in shaping our environment through agreement.

Your words:

- Shape how you see yourself.
- Shape how others perceive you.
- Shape your confidence.

- Shape your expectations.
- Shape your actions.

If you constantly say, “I’m overwhelmed,” your body responds as if you are defeated. If you constantly say, “Nothing ever works for me,” you’re thinking narrows, and you stop looking for solutions. But if you say, “I am learning,” your brain looks for growth. If you say, “God is giving me strategy,” your mind searches for answers. Your mouth trains your mind. And your mind directs your movement.

Dominion Starts in the Heart

You cannot consistently speak beyond what you believe. If you want your words to change, your heart must change. If you want your manifestation to change, your meditation must change. Guard your heart. Feed it truth. Renew your mind. Because when your heart is full of alignment, your mouth becomes an instrument of authority. Then “you shall have what you say” stops being motivational — and starts being visible.

You begin to:

Speak peace and carry it.
Speak structure and build it.
Speak discipline and practice it.
Speak expansion and prepare for it.

Not because you are pretending. But because your heart has been governed. You do not rise to the level of your declarations alone. You rise to the level of your internal abundance. If you want different outcomes, fill your heart differently. If you want stronger authority, store stronger truth. If you want sustainable territory, align your heart with Heaven. Because the mouth speaks what the heart stores. And eventually you live what you repeatedly say.

Reprogramming the Heart

Renewing the Mind

Scripture Foundation

Romans 12:2 (KJV)
"Be not conformed to this world: but be ye transformed by the renewing of your mind..."

Proverbs 23:7 (KJV)
"For as he thinketh in his heart, so is he..."

2 Corinthians 10:5 (KJV)
"Casting down imaginations... bringing into captivity every thought..."

If you are going to have what you say, and your mouth speaks from your heart, then the real work is not only in your speech. It is in your storage system. The heart stores what the mind repeatedly entertains. And whatever is stored becomes abundance. Reprogramming your heart is not emotional hype. It is disciplined mental renovation.

Step 1: Audit What You Are Feeding Your Mind

You cannot renew a mind you refuse to monitor.

Ask yourself:

What do I think about consistently?
What narratives replay in my head?
What do I consume daily — conversations, media, environments?

Your mind is shaped by repetition. If you constantly consume negativity, comparison, drama, or scarcity — your heart will store it. Renewal begins with exposure control. If it weakens your faith, limit it. If it distorts your focus, remove it. If it contradicts your assignment, guard against it. You cannot build dominion while feeding dysfunction.

Step 2: Replace, Don't Just Remove

Many people try to "stop thinking negatively" without replacing the thought. But empty space invites old patterns back. Renewal is replacement. When fear speaks, answer it with truth. When insecurity surfaces, confront it with identity. When scarcity appears, rehearse stewardship and provision. This is what 2 Corinthians 10:5 means by taking thoughts captive. You do not negotiate with every thought. You arrest it.

You ask:

Does this align with who God says I am?
Does this support my calling?
Does this build capacity?

If not replace it.

Step 3: Speak What You Want to Store

The heart stores what is repeated with emotion. This is why confession matters. When you consistently declare:

"I am disciplined."
"I am growing."
"I have a sound mind."
"I steward well."

You are not pretending. You are programming. Repetition forms belief. Belief forms identity. Identity forms behavior. Eventually, what started as intentional confession becomes natural conviction.

Step 4: Align Environment with Renewal

You cannot renew your mind while living in constant mental clutter.

Renewal requires:

• Quiet moments.
• Focused time.
• Structured habits.
• Intentional community.

Your environment either reinforces old patterns or supports new ones. If you want a renewed mind, build renewed rhythms. Start your day with truth before noise. Write vision before scrolling. Pray before reacting. Plan before responding. Renewal is daily not occasional.

Step 5: Practice Mental Discipline Under Pressure

It is easy to think clearly when life is calm. Renewal is proven under pressure. When stress comes, do you revert to old thinking? Or do you stand on what you've been storing? Pressure reveals programming. If panic surfaces quickly, more renewal is required. If clarity remains steady, renewal is working. Reprogramming the heart is not instant. It is consistent. Just like physical training strengthens muscles, mental discipline strengthens thinking.

What Happens When the Mind Is Renewed

When your mind is renewed:

• You stop self-sabotaging opportunities.
• You stop shrinking in rooms you prayed for.
• You stop speaking defeat over situations.
• You start anticipating strategy instead of assuming failure.
• You move with calm authority instead of emotional reaction.

Slowly your heart shifts. Fear decreases. Confidence increases. Clarity stabilizes. Vision strengthens. Then your mouth changes naturally. And when your mouth changes, your direction changes.

You do not transform by accident. You transform by renewal. Renewal is not a feeling. It is a decision repeated daily.

Guard what enters your mind. Replace what contradicts truth.Repeat what aligns with your assignment. Build environments that reinforce growth.
Stand firm under pressure, because as you think in your heart, so you become. And as you become, so you speak. And as you speak, so you build.

Purposed to Dominate

Scripture Foundation

Jeremiah 1:5 (KJV)
"Before I formed thee in the belly I knew thee; and before thou camest forth out of the womb I sanctified thee..."

Genesis 1:28 (KJV)
"...Be fruitful, and multiply... and have dominion..."

Ephesians 2:10 (KJV)
"For we are his workmanship, created in Christ Jesus unto good works, which God hath before ordained that we should walk in them."

John 15:8 (KJV)
"Herein is my Father glorified, that ye bear much fruit; so shall ye be my disciples."

To be purposed to dominate does not mean you are called to overpower people. It means you are designed to excel, establish order, and bear fruit in the specific sphere God assigned to you. Dominion is not random. It is territorial. And territory is connected to purpose. Before you were formed, you were known. Before you were born, you were set apart. That means your assignment existed before your arrival. Dominion is not self-created ambition. It is divine authorization.

Dominion Is Proven by Fruit

John 15:8 reveals something powerful:

The Father is glorified when you bear much fruit. Not little fruit. Not occasional fruit. Much fruit. Fruit is evidence of alignment. Fruit is proof of health. Fruit is the visible result of invisible connection. To dominate in your assigned area means to produce consistent, measurable impact there. If you are called to lead — fruit looks like growth, stability, development in those you oversee. If you are called to business — fruit looks like systems, sustainability, ethical increase. If you are called to ministry — fruit looks like transformed lives, clarity, spiritual maturity. Dominion without fruit is noise. True dominion produces results. And those results glorify God. You are not called to dominate for recognition. You are called to dominate so that your excellence points back to Him.

Dominion Is Sphere-Specific

Many become frustrated because they attempt to dominate in areas they were never assigned to. They compare mantles. They chase platforms.
They imitate callings. But dominion flows where you are planted. A seed only bears fruit in proper soil. If you are planted in business, dominate there. If you are planted in leadership, dominate there. If you are planted in creative expression, dominate there. Your grace is territorial. When you function in your assigned sphere, things respond differently. Clarity increases.

Ideas flow. Momentum builds. Because you are operating within divine design.

To Dominate Means to Establish Standard

Being purposed to dominate means you are not called to blend into dysfunction. You are called to elevate environments. Dominion introduces order. It builds structure where there was chaos. It strengthens integrity where there was compromise. It raises excellence where there was mediocrity. You do not dominate through aggression. You dominate through consistency, clarity, and fruit. And fruit becomes undeniable. People may ignore words. They cannot ignore results.

Dominion Requires Responsibility

Genesis commands fruitfulness before dominion. Be fruitful. Multiply. Then have dominion. Fruit proves readiness. If you cannot produce in small spaces, you are not ready for larger ones. John 15 makes it clear: fruitfulness glorifies the Father. That means your capacity to produce is spiritual responsibility. You are not just managing a career. You are stewarding an assignment. You are not just building influence. You are bearing fruit that reflects Heaven.

To be purposed to dominate means:

- You take ownership of growth.
- You refine your craft continually.

- You build instead of complain.
- You produce instead of perform.

Because fruit sustains territory. You were not created to survive your calling. You were designed to establish it. You are purposed to dominate in your assigned area — not through control, but through fruit. Not through ego, but through excellence. Not through noise, but through results. And when you bear much fruit in your territory — The Father is glorified.

Dominion is not about you being seen. It is about God being revealed through what you produce. When purpose aligns with preparation, and capacity supports character — Dominion becomes natural. Because you are not striving. You are simply functioning in what you were designed to do.

Prophetic Declaration

I Bear Fruit in My Territory

Scripture Foundation

John 15:8 (KJV)
"Herein is my Father glorified, that ye bear much fruit..."

Genesis 1:28 (KJV)
"Be fruitful, and multiply... and have dominion..."

Psalm 1:3 (KJV)
"And he shall be like a tree planted by the rivers of water, that bringeth forth his fruit in his season..."

Colossians 1:10 (KJV)
"...being fruitful in every good work, and increasing in the knowledge of God."

Today I stand in agreement with my assignment.

I am not misplaced.
I am not random.
I am planted with purpose.

Purposed to Dominate

And I bear fruit in my territory.

Your Word declares that You are glorified when I bear much fruit
so I reject barrenness in the area You called me to.

I will not shrink in my assignment.
I will not produce below my design.
I will not function beneath my capacity. I am fruitful.

In my leadership I produce growth.
In my business I produce sustainability.
In my ministry I produce transformation.
In my discipline I produce consistency.
In my thinking I produce clarity.

I am like a tree planted by living water.

I do not strive for fruit
I remain connected and fruit follows.

Where I am planted, I prosper.

Where I am assigned, I build.

Where I am called, I establish.

I reject distraction from my territory.

I refuse comparison with another's assignment.

I dominate where I am designed.

Purposed to Dominate

My work multiplies.
My influence expands.
My systems strengthen.
My roots deepen.

I produce results that glorify God. I produce solutions where there were problems. I produce order where there was chaos.
I produce excellence where there was mediocrity.

Fruit flows from my obedience.
Fruit flows from my discipline.
Fruit flows from my connection to Christ.

I will not be barren in a place I was graced for.

I will not be unproductive in a place I was purposed for.

I bear fruit in my territory.

And as I remain faithful,
my fruit will multiply.

In Jesus' name,
Amen.

Dominion Is Lived, Not Announced

Dominion was never about ego. It was never about control, visibility, or superiority. It was always about stewardship. From the beginning, God created humanity in His image and gave them dominion. That order matters. Image first. Authority second. Character before capacity. Alignment before expansion. You have learned that dominion is responsibility. It requires internal governance before external influence. It demands discipline before enlargement. It insists on capacity before territory.

You cannot dominate externally what you refuse to govern internally. Your atmosphere must be ordered. Your thinking must be sharpened. Your heart must be aligned. Your words must agree with truth. Your systems must support growth. Because you will have what you say, but you will say what fills your heart. And if your heart is governed, your life will follow. Dominion is not loud. It is structured. It is visible in fruit. Jesus said the Father is glorified when you bear much fruit.

That means dominion is not proven by title it is proven by results. Fruit proves alignment. Fruit proves connection. Fruit proves maturity. You were purposed to dominate not everywhere, but somewhere. You are assigned to a territory. A sphere. A responsibility. A field that carries your name in Heaven's blueprint. And in that territory, you are not called to survive. You are called to establish. To bring order. To raise standards. To build systems. To create sustainability. To multiply what has been entrusted to you.

But territory only expands where capacity is strengthened. And preparation is proof that you believe expansion is coming.

So, you prepare. You build. You refine. You renew. You strengthen.
You align. Because dominion is not seized. It is sustained. And sustained dominion glorifies God. You do not dominate for applause. You dominate through obedience. You do not dominate by force. You dominate by fruit. You do not dominate by striving. You dominate by alignment.

When your interior is strong, your exterior can grow.
When your thinking is renewed, your speech carries authority.
When your heart is aligned, your life becomes stable.
When your capacity expands, your territory follows.
When your preparation is consistent, opportunity recognizes you.

Dominion is lived, not announced. It is the quiet confidence of someone who knows they are assigned.
It is the discipline of someone who understands responsibility.
It is the fruit of someone who remains connected.

You are not here by accident. You are not carrying vision randomly. You are not driven without design. You are purposed. And in your assigned territory, when you walk in discipline, alignment, and obedience —

Dominion becomes inevitable.

The Law of Multiplication

Designed to Multiply

Scripture Foundation

Genesis 1:28 (KJV)
"Be fruitful, and multiply..."

John 15:16 (KJV)
"...I have chosen you... that ye should go and bring forth fruit, and that your fruit should remain..."

2 Corinthians 9:10 (KJV)
"Now he that ministereth seed to the sower both minister bread for your food, and multiply your seed sown..."

Dominion establishes. Multiplication expands. From the very beginning, God did not simply command fruitfulness. He commanded multiplication. Fruitfulness proves you can produce. Multiplication proves you can steward.

There is a difference. Fruitfulness is the ability to create results. Multiplication is the ability to reproduce results consistently, sustainably, and beyond yourself. You were never designed to stop at success. You were designed to reproduce impact.

Multiplication Is a Kingdom Law

In the natural world, everything God created carries the capacity to multiply.
Seeds multiply.
Trees multiply.
Animals multiply.
Ideas multiply.
Influence multiplies.

The Kingdom operates on increase. God does not think in addition. He thinks in multiplication. Addition increases by one. Multiplication increases by capacity.

If you only think in addition, you will constantly exhaust yourself trying to grow incrementally.

But when you understand multiplication, you begin building systems, people, and structures that reproduce without constant strain.

Fruit That Remains

Jesus said not only to bear fruit, but fruit that remains. Remaining fruit is sustained impact.

It means:

- Your systems continue without collapse.
- Your leadership produces leaders.

• Your teaching produces maturity.
• Your business outlives emotional seasons.
• Your discipline creates generational stability.

Multiplication is not momentary growth. It is durable expansion. It is growth that does not disappear when pressure increases.

Multiplication Requires Seed

Second Corinthians says God multiplies seed sown.

Notice: He multiplies seed not stored potential.

Multiplication requires release. You cannot multiply what you refuse to sow.

If you hoard knowledge, it stops with you.
If you withhold leadership, it ends with you.
If you resist delegation, growth stalls.

Seed must leave your hand to multiply.

Multiplication is activated by generosity, investment, and release.

Multiplication Requires Structure

Multiplication without structure leads to chaos. Growth without systems leads to burnout. If God multiplies what you have built, can your structure sustain it? If influence doubles, can your discipline handle it? If revenue increases, can your stewardship manage it? Multiplication magnifies everything including weaknesses. That is why dominion and capacity had to come first. Multiplication rests on what you have already strengthened.

You Are Called to Reproduce What You Carry

Multiplication is not only about money or numbers. It is about influence. You reproduce what you consistently embody.

If you carry clarity, you reproduce clarity.
If you carry discipline, you reproduce discipline.
If you carry excellence, you reproduce excellence.

If you carry confusion, you reproduce confusion.
If you carry instability, you reproduce instability.

Multiplication reveals what is truly within you.

So, the question is not, "Do I want increase?"

The question is, "What am I currently positioned to multiply?"

God did not call you just to build something successful. He called you to build something that multiplies. Not just fruit. But fruit that remains.

Multiplication means your impact extends beyond your effort.

It means your systems outlive your emotions.

It means your influence outgrows your presence. It means what you built continues producing long after you step back.

Dominion establishes.
Capacity strengthens.
Preparation stabilizes.
Fruit proves.
Multiplication expands.

When multiplication begins Your territory no longer depends solely on you. It becomes self-sustaining. That is Kingdom growth.

Prophetic Declaration

I Am Built to Multiply

Scripture Foundation

Genesis 1:28 (KJV)
"Be fruitful, and multiply..."

John 15:16 (KJV)
"...that ye should go and bring forth fruit, and that your fruit should remain..."

2 Corinthians 9:10 (KJV)
"...and multiply your seed sown..."

Ecclesiastes 11:6 (KJV)
"In the morning sow thy seed... for thou knowest not whether shall prosper, either this or that, or whether they both shall be alike good."

Today I come into agreement with Heaven's design for my life.

I am not created merely to produce
I am created to multiply.

Purposed to Dominate

I reject small thinking.
I reject survival mentality.
I reject the belief that increase is accidental.

I am built to multiply.

Where I sow, growth follows.
Where I build, expansion begins.
Where I invest, reproduction occurs.

I do not hoard what God placed in my hands.
I release it in faith.

I sow wisdom.
I sow discipline.
I sow structure.
I sow leadership.
I sow generosity.

And God multiplies my seed.

My fruit does not disappear after one season.

It remains.

My systems are sustainable.
My leadership reproduces leaders.
My influence creates influence.
My discipline produces consistency in others.

I am not overwhelmed by increase.

I am structured for it.

Purposed to Dominate

As territory expands, my capacity expands.
As responsibility grows, my wisdom grows.
As influence increases, my integrity deepens.

Multiplication does not intimidate me.

It confirms me.

I am planted to flourish.
I am disciplined to sustain.
I am aligned to expand.

What God has placed in me will not stop with me.

It will grow beyond me.

My work multiplies.
My impact multiplies.
My obedience multiplies.
My stewardship multiplies.

I am built to multiply not for ego,
but for impact.

Not for applause,
but for legacy.

And as I remain faithful,
He multiplies what I sow.

In Jesus' name,
Amen

Chapter 11

Prayers for Dominion, Capacity, and Multiplication

Scripture Foundation

Luke 10:19 (KJV)
"Behold, I give unto you power... over all the power of the enemy..."

James 1:5 (KJV)
"If any of you lack wisdom, let him ask of God..."

Psalm 90:17 (KJV)
"And let the beauty of the Lord our God be upon us: and establish thou the work of our hands..."

Prayer for Alignment With My Assignment

Father, in the name of Jesus,

I thank You that my life is not accidental. You formed me with intention and purpose. According to Your Word in **Jeremiah 1:5**, You knew me before I was formed in the womb.

Today I ask that You align my heart with the assignment You have given me.

Remove every distraction that pulls me away from my purpose. Silence every voice that contradicts Your direction for my life. Give me clarity to recognize the territory You have called me to influence.

Let my desires align with Your will. Let my actions reflect Your wisdom. Let my life reflect Your design.

Teach me to walk confidently in the area where You have called me to dominate.

In Jesus' name,
Amen.

Prayer for a Renewed Mind

Father,

Your Word says in **Romans 12:2** that transformation comes through the renewing of the mind.

So today I surrender my thinking to You.

Renew my mind where it has been limited.
Correct my thinking where it has been distorted.
Replace fear with faith.

Replace confusion with clarity.
Replace insecurity with identity.

Help me take every thought captive according to **2 Corinthians 10:5**.

Teach me to think strategically, to discern wisely, and to see opportunities through the lens of Your truth.

Sharpen my thinking so my decisions reflect wisdom.

Let my mind become a place where vision, clarity, and faith grow strong.

In Jesus' name,
Amen.

Prayer for Discipline and Capacity

Lord,

Your Word says in **Luke 16:10** that he who is faithful in little will be faithful in much.

So before I ask for more territory, I ask You to strengthen my capacity.

Develop discipline within me.
Teach me consistency in the unseen places.
Give me the strength to build what You have shown me.

Strengthen my character so influence does not corrupt me.
Strengthen my habits so success does not overwhelm me.
Strengthen my endurance so pressure does not break me.

Increase my ability to steward what You place in my hands.

Build my interior so my exterior can grow.

In Jesus' name,
Amen.

Prayer to Govern My Atmosphere

Father,

Your Word says in **Proverbs 4:23** to guard the heart diligently because the issues of life flow from it.

Teach me to govern my atmosphere.

Give me wisdom to remove what weakens my focus.
Give me courage to confront what disrupts order.
Give me discernment to recognize influences that distract me from my assignment.

Let peace rule in my environment.

Let clarity guide my decisions.

Let discipline define my daily rhythms.

May my atmosphere become a place where vision thrives and productivity grows.

In Jesus' name,
Amen.

Prayer for Fruitfulness

Father,

Jesus said in **John 15:8** that You are glorified when we bear much fruit.

So, I ask You to make my life fruitful.

Let the work of my hands produce results.
Let the seeds I sow grow into lasting impact.
Let the systems I build create stability.

Where there has been delay, release fruit.

Where there has been stagnation, release growth.

Help me remain connected to You so my fruit remains.

May my life reflect productivity, excellence, and faithful stewardship.

In Jesus' name,
Amen.

Prayer for Multiplication

Lord,

You commanded in **Genesis 1:28** to be fruitful and multiply.

So, I ask You to multiply what You have placed in my hands.

Multiply my wisdom.
Multiply my influence.
Multiply my opportunities.
Multiply my resources.

Let my impact extend beyond my effort.

Teach me how to build systems that grow.

Teach me how to lead people who lead others.

Teach me how to sow seeds that produce generational results.

Let my life produce fruit that remains.

In Jesus' name,
Amen.

Prayer for Legacy

Father,

I do not want my life to end with temporary success. I want to build something that lasts.

According to **Psalm 90:17**, establish the work of my hands. Let what I build carry integrity. Let what I build carry wisdom. Let what I build carry influence that points back to You. May the seeds I plant bless generations I may never meet.

Let my life reflect faithful stewardship of the assignment You gave me.

In Jesus' name,
Amen.

Closing Prayer

Father, Thank You for trusting me with purpose. Help me walk in dominion with humility.
Help me carry responsibility with wisdom.
Help me steward influence with integrity.

Strengthen my interior. Expand my capacity. Multiply what I sow. And let my life bring glory to Your name. In Jesus' name,
Amen.

The Prayer of Dominion

Scripture Foundation

Genesis 1:28 (KJV)
"...Be fruitful, and multiply... and have dominion..."

Luke 10:19 (KJV)
"Behold, I give unto you power... over all the power of the enemy..."

Psalm 90:17 (KJV)
"Let the beauty of the Lord our God be upon us: and establish thou the work of our hands..."

John 15:8 (KJV)
"Herein is my Father glorified, that ye bear much fruit..."

Heavenly Father,

I come before You with humility and gratitude, recognizing that every gift, every opportunity, and every assignment in my life comes from You.

You created me with purpose.
You designed me with intention.
And according to Your Word, You have given me dominion.

Today I receive the responsibility of that dominion.

Not as power for my own glory, but as stewardship for Your Kingdom.

Father, align my heart with Your will.

Let my thoughts reflect Your wisdom.
Let my words reflect Your truth.
Let my actions reflect Your character.

Strengthen my interior so my life can carry the weight of the assignment You have placed on me.

Renew my mind so I think with clarity and discernment.

Guard my heart so that what flows from it produces life.

Teach me to govern my atmosphere with discipline, peace, and order.

Where there has been confusion, bring clarity.
Where there has been fear, release courage.
Where there has been limitation, release vision.

Father, make me fruitful.

Let the work of my hands produce lasting impact.
Let the seeds I sow grow into something greater than I imagined.
Let what I build bring stability, blessing, and opportunity to others.

Purposed to Dominate

According to Your Word, let my fruit remain.

Help me steward what You have given me with integrity.

Where I need wisdom, grant it generously.
Where I need discipline, strengthen me.
Where I need healing, restore me. Expand my capacity so I can carry what You release.

Multiply the seeds I sow. Multiply my influence for good. Multiply my leadership to develop others. Multiply the impact of my obedience.

Let what You have placed in my life grow beyond me.

Establish the work of my hands.

Build through me what will outlast me.

Let my life be evidence of Your goodness.

Let my leadership reflect Your order.

Let my fruit bring You glory.

And wherever You have assigned me —

Help me to walk in dominion with humility,
with wisdom,
with discipline,
and with faith.

Purposed to Dominate

Not striving for recognition,
but faithfully stewarding what You have entrusted to me.

May my life produce fruit.
May my work multiply.
May my obedience create legacy.

And may everything I build point back to You.

In Jesus' name,

Amen.

Now Go and Take Your Territory

Scripture Foundation

Joshua 1:3 (KJV)
"Every place that the sole of your foot shall tread upon, that have I given unto you..."

Deuteronomy 28:13 (KJV)
"And the Lord shall make thee the head, and not the tail..."

Romans 5:17 (KJV)
"...they which receive abundance of grace... shall reign in life by one, Jesus Christ."

You have read the principles. You have reflected on the truths. You have prayed the prayers. Now comes the moment where revelation becomes responsibility. This is where faith becomes action. You were never meant to simply read about dominion. You were meant to walk in it.

From the beginning, God created you with intention. He formed you with purpose and placed within you the capacity to influence, build, steward, and multiply.

Dominion was never meant to remain a concept. It was meant to become a lifestyle.

Throughout this journey you have learned that dominion begins internally. Your thinking must be renewed. Your heart must be aligned. Your atmosphere must be governed.

You have discovered that capacity determines territory. Preparation proves faith. Fruit reveals alignment. And multiplication expands what has been faithfully built. All of these truths lead to this moment.

The moment where you stop waiting for permission. The moment where you stop shrinking in places you were assigned to influence.

The moment where you stop minimizing what God placed inside you.

Joshua was told that every place his foot stepped had already been given to him. The territory was promised, but it still required movement. The same is true for you.

Some doors will open because you prayed. But many doors will open because you prepared.

Some opportunities will come because of favor. But many opportunities will come because you built the capacity to carry them.

Dominion is not passive. It is intentional. It is walking into your assignment with discipline, clarity, and faith. It is building systems where there was disorder. It is raising standards where there was compromise. It is producing fruit where there was stagnation. And doing it all with humility, wisdom, and stewardship. Your territory may be a business. It may be a ministry. It may be leadership within an organization. It may be influence within your community. It may be ideas, creativity, innovation, or solutions that God has placed within you. Whatever your territory is, it carries responsibility. And you have been prepared to carry it. Not because you are perfect, but because you are willing.

Willing to grow. Willing to learn. Willing to steward what God places in your hands, and when you walk in that posture, dominion becomes natural. Not forced. Not arrogant. Not self-promoting. But evident. Because fruit will follow.

So now I leave you with this charge:

Guard your heart. Renew your mind. Strengthen your capacity. Prepare with discipline. Produce fruit in your territory. Multiply what God has entrusted to you. Walk confidently in the assignment Heaven has placed on your life. You are not here to survive your purpose. You are here to establish it. Now go and take your territory.

Take time to prayerfully reflect on the journey you have taken through this book. Use these questions for personal reflection, journaling, or group discussion.

1. What area of your life do you believe God has assigned you to influence or steward? What does dominion look like in that territory?
2. In what ways has your thinking limited your growth, and what steps can you take to renew your mind according to Romans 12:2?
3. What environments or influences in your life may be affecting your atmosphere? How can you begin to govern your atmosphere more intentionally?
4. Where might God be calling you to strengthen your capacity before expanding your territory?
5. What areas of your life require greater discipline and preparation so you can steward what God entrusts to you?
6. What fruit do you see in your life today that reflects alignment with your purpose?
7. What seeds are you currently sowing that could produce multiplication in the future?
8. How can you develop systems, habits, or structures that allow your work to grow beyond your individual effort?
9. What is one step you can take this week to move closer to the territory God has assigned to you?
10. How will you remain connected to God so that the fruit you produce continues to grow and remain?

Take time to pray, write, and reflect on what God is revealing to you. Dominion is not simply learned—it is lived through daily obedience, faith, and stewardship.

The 30-Day Dominion Challenge

Dominion is not simply something we understand—it is something we practice daily.

This 30-Day Dominion Challenge is designed to help you apply the principles from this book in your daily life. Each day focuses on strengthening your thinking, aligning your heart, building your capacity, and walking confidently in the territory God has assigned to you.

Take a few moments each day to reflect, pray, and apply the focus for that day.

Day 1 — Reflect on the territory God has assigned to your life. Ask Him for clarity about where you are called to influence.

Day 2 — Read Genesis 1:28 and meditate on what it means to be fruitful and walk in dominion.

Day 3 — Examine your thinking. Identify any beliefs that may be limiting your growth.

Day 4 — Speak life over your future. Declare God's promises over your life and assignment.

Day 5 — Evaluate your daily habits. What habits support your purpose and what habits need to change?

Day 6 — Take time to pray for wisdom and clarity in the decisions you are currently facing.

Day 7 — Remove one distraction from your life that is pulling you away from your purpose.

Day 8 — Ask God to reveal areas where you need to grow in discipline.

Day 9 — Strengthen your atmosphere. Create space for prayer, reflection, and focus.

Day 10 — Identify one skill or area of knowledge you can begin developing to strengthen your capacity.

Day 11 — Reflect on Luke 16:10 and commit to being faithful in the small responsibilities you already have.

Day 12 — Write down three ways you can improve your stewardship of time, resources, or influence.

Day 13 — Pray for courage to step into opportunities God places before you.

Day 14 — Speak declarations of faith over your life and your territory.

Day 15 — Reflect on John 15:8 and ask God to help your life bear fruit that remains.

Day 16 — Evaluate your environment. Are the people and influences around you strengthening your purpose?

Day 17 — Identify one area where you can serve or contribute to others.

Day 18 — Take one step toward building something that aligns with your purpose.

Day 19 — Reflect on your progress so far and thank God for the growth you are experiencing.

Day 20 — Ask God to increase your capacity to steward influence and opportunity.

Day 21 — Speak gratitude over your life and the territory God has entrusted to you.

Day 22 — Write down new ideas or strategies God has placed on your heart.

Day 23 — Strengthen your discipline by committing to one positive daily habit.

Day 24 — Pray for wisdom in leadership and decision-making.

Day 25 — Reflect on how your thinking has begun to change over the past weeks.

Day 26 — Identify ways your life can produce fruit that benefits others.

Day 27 — Ask God to multiply the seeds you have sown.

Day 28 — Reflect on the impact you want your life to have in the years ahead.

Day 29 — Thank God for preparing you to walk confidently in your territory.

Day 30 — Pray the Prayer of Dominion and recommit your life to stewarding your purpose faithfully.

Dominion is not achieved in a moment—it is developed through daily alignment, discipline, and obedience.

Continue walking in your assignment, building with wisdom, and trusting God to multiply what He has placed in your hands.

The Author's Blessing

Before you close this book, I want to speak a blessing over your life.

May the God who created you with purpose strengthen your heart and renew your mind. May you walk confidently in the territory He has assigned to you and steward every opportunity placed in your hands with wisdom and integrity.

May your thinking be sharpened and your vision made clear. May every seed you sow produce fruit that remains, and may the work of your hands be established according to the will of God.

I pray that you grow in discipline, clarity, and spiritual maturity. That where there has been confusion, God will release direction. Where there has been hesitation, He will release courage. Where there has been limitation, He will expand your capacity.

May your life bear fruit that glorifies God.

May your influence strengthen others.

May your leadership bring order where there was once disorder.

May what you build multiply and create impact beyond your lifetime.

According to **Psalm 90:17**, may the favor of the Lord rest upon you, and may He establish the work of your hands.

According to **John 15:8**, may your life bear much fruit. According to **Genesis 1:28**, may you walk in fruitfulness, multiplication, and dominion. As you go forward from this moment, may you carry the responsibility of your calling with humility and faith.

May your territory expand as your capacity grows. May everything you build reflect the goodness and wisdom of God. Walk boldly in your assignment. Produce fruit in your territory. Multiply what God has placed within you. You were created with purpose, and you are purposed to dominate.

Minister Darlene Bell

www.ingramcontent.com/pod-product-compliance
Lightning Source LLC
LaVergne TN
LVHW090526110826
845146LV00003B/996

* 9 7 9 8 9 9 5 4 0 2 7 0 1 *